21 Days of Training

Aaron Tucker

Personalized Dog Training

Table of Contents

Table of Contents

Opening Thoughts

Welcome to the wonderful world of dog training, where everyone you meet on the street is all of a sudden a pro and knows what's best for you and your dog.

I believe dog training is what it is and needs to be simple to the point, and fun. I don't use big fancy words or try to over complicate any behavior that we are working on. A 'sit' is a 'sit' in any language. I wrote this intending it to be more of a daily guide rather than a book. Let's face it, did you buy this wanting to hear the stories of my days on SWAT doing dynamic entries? Or my days as Cadaver K9 handler doing body recovery missions? Yeah, I didn't think so. You just want to train your dog. If you want to hear about how I was homeless in high school and slept on a bench at a church working at a kennel and eating from the dumpster behind a local grocery store we can talk about that somewhere else. We are here to train dogs, not make a life time movie or write a country song.

The training within this book is structured over a 21-day timeline in which I break down how to create habits and train your dog day by day. When you create a habit, your dog will as well. You just might find yourself wanting more and looking for new goals to achieve with your dog. I highly encourage all my clients to keep challenging themselves and their dogs. Look for local clubs and getting involved in competitions. It is not only fun but also pushes you to sharpen your skills and builds the bond between you and your dog. I have provided space in each training section for you to put notes and track your progress if you'd like. I found this to be very helpful when training my own dogs, as it allows you to go back and see the progress. Of course, I highly suggest recording yourself training as well. I do it all the time and you can see first-hand the improvements you and your dog make, and also where you as a human mess up. Yes, we all mess up accept it and move on. Even better, laugh and learn, then come back and crush it.

So enough about all that let get to this! The first part of this book is a quick introduction in how to create leadership. Look at this as set of ground rules to help you define your role to your dog. Then we get right into the training. Each day is broken into small training sessions. The goal is to space each one out throughout the day getting a total of 30 minutes of training each day. Keeping the training sessions short keeps the dog wanting more and preventing the dog from getting bored with it. There is enough space for you to write notes and track your progress as you train.

The terminology is going to be simple and to the point; I don't believe in tones of commands. I believe in focusing on the basics. Follow the 'KISS' method: Keep it Stupid Simple. If you follow this mind set and break each behavior down to the smallest movements, you will find yourself with the ability to teach your dog anything.

Always Remember My 2 Laws Of Dog Training

1. Who's dog is this? It's your dog, so train the dog to be your dog. If a technique isn't working and you feel like its hindering your relationship stop and find an alternative.

2. HAVE FUN!!!! Having a dog is like having a best friend and you have fun with your best friend. So, if you aren't having fun, we are doing it wrong and we need change our training method.

Establishing Leadership Is Not Done By Force

It is not necessary to apply physical force in order to establish yourself as the dog's leader and therefore the dominant figure of your team. When and if force is used it is never used with emotion. Calm assertive energy must always be used.

Dogs have active defense reflexes which mean they may react to physical pain and aggressive emotion by striking out defensively. Passive dogs may shut down and be afraid to move or think. You do not want to cause your dog to react this way, so avoid using physical force to establish leadership.

To Establish Dominance:

Think like a dog and apply the same rules that dogs use to govern themselves

1. Let your dog see you eat something before feeding. Most people feed their dogs before they eat. The dog that gets to eat first is the pack leader in the dog world. Do not free feed your dog. The dog must look to you for sustenance of life. The dog must be calm and submissive before the food his given "sit" is a good exercise to practice until you allow the dog to eat.

2. Have your dog enter and exit your house behind you. You first then the dog. This is the same for stairs. Never allow your dog to go to the top of the stairs and watch you come up to them. Your head is

lowered watching your feet as you approach and your dog's head is elevated in a position over yours.

3. Go for at least 2 walks a day. The length of the walk depends on the energy level of you and your dog. Wolf packs migrate for close to 15 miles a day in the wild. You are the leader of this walk. Stop and let your dog sniff and pee at intervals, not when you want them to, must be your decision on where to sniff and where to pee.

4. Do not allow your dog to initiate all play activity. You play when you want to and not at your dog's request. Tell the dog to down and wait a while before you play. Make sure all games are controlled by you. Your dog must have a release command before you play any tug games. If you are not strong enough to control your dog don't play tug games.

5. Petting is a big training tool. When your dog asks for attention, have he/she to do something for it. For example; Sit first or lie down. Don't constantly pet your dog while you are in a training session. Use petting as a reward. Why would we work for something we get all the time? Be sure of what state of mind you are reinforcing with your petting. If your dog is scared, aggressive, or out of control you should not be petting your dog.

6. When my dog is being obnoxious and refuses to respond to me, I put my dogs in a calm submissive state with my voice and body language moving towards to the dog. If this doesn't work, I simply put the dog in the crate for a little while. I don't yell or fuss or handle the dog harshly. Just put the dog away. When the dog and you have calmed down let the dog out. Don't make a big deal when you let the dog out just let the dog out though.

7. The dog sleeps in its space and you sleep in your space. If you let your dog sleep in your bed or chairs, you are placing yourself as his

sibling or equal. Be sure to sit in its place from time to time. If you are going to allow your dog on the bed or the couch, make sure you are taking control of the space. This mean you sit on the couch and invite the dog up. If the dog is on the couch and you come in to sit on the couch, simply calmly have the dog get down from the couch before you sit down. Once the dog is on the ground and you are sitting you can now invite the dog back up to the couch. The same goes for the bed.

8. Don't constantly let your dog in and out of the house on its request. Know when the last time it had a chance to go to the bathroom was. Tell it to wait and them out on your initiative. While toilet training, it's smart and let the puppy out whenever it asks. Puppies have to go a lot.

9. Being pushy about your attention is a form of dominance. Pet me when I want to be petted. Let me out whenever I want to go out. Play with me when I want you to. When the dog makes any attempt to mouth arms, hands, or any part of the body clothing, or leash give a loud command of 'OFF' with the most piercing eye contact that you can. No praise should be given when the dog stops.

10. After your dog has been socialized and is friendly and outgoing towards people, do not allow it to greet strangers before you do. Leaders always greet strangers first and decide who is a friend or who isn't. You want that to be you and not your dog. Teach your dog from puppy hood, to sit and accept praise and petting. It is in this position that the dog meets people. If your dog is shy, do not force this on him. Tell whoever is approaching you to please ignore your dog. You greet the stranger and let the puppy sniff him. If the stranger goes straight for your shy dog, the dog may back away or maybe try and ward the stranger off with an aggressive display. Your dog should not be barking at the stranger and that you stop by

putting the dog in a submissive state. I use the 'lay down' command for instances such as this.

Crate Training

Let's start here with one of the simplest tools that will save your dog and your house. Crate training. Some live by it. Some well that just don't do it. Crate training in my opinion is an absolute must if you have a dog. Crate training does not mean your dog lives in its crate. You don't live in your bedroom. But you have your own room that is your place to get away and relax. That is what you are teaching your dog. Dogs are den animals so at stressful times they will retreat to a safe area. That's what you are giving them with a crate. We want to make the crate as positive of a place as we possibly can.

Crate training is easier than most people think. I won't lie, it does take a little tough love, but once the dog accepts the crate, they will love it. I will not just crate the dog when I leave the house, I will even crate train them when I am home watching a tv show. The key is that the dog doesn't look at the crate as a sign you are leaving for a long period of time. Whenever you put the dog in the crate, you act the same whether you are just running out to check the mail or you going to be gone for a couple hours. When you get home, you act the same as well. I never let the dog out while its barking or whining. If the dog is quiet I simply calmly just let the dog out. Do not make a big deal about it. Not one makes a big deal about you coming out of your room when you get up in the morning.

This is how simple it is. Take a KONG, take some wet dog food and some of your dog's kibble mix it up. Fill the KONG with it and then freeze it. Now every time you put the dog in the crate, give them the KONG and only give them the KONG when you are putting them in the crate. If you do this for a while you will notice every time you go to the freezer you will probably find your dog running to the crate asking to be let into it.

Crate training is done whenever you can't physically watch your dog. If you can't see them or have to step out for a minute, put them in the crate. As the dog gets older and earns your trust that it can be loose in the house unsupervised without being destructive, then you can let them be out. I still have my crates up even though my older dogs are free all the time. I will still find them sleeping in them with the doors open.

If the dog is very young you may have to avoid bedding in the crate because they could shred it and ingest it. Once they are out of that stage. I put a bed back in the crate.

Potty Training

Oh, the dreaded potty or house breaking training. There is no way around accidents, so just suck it up and accept that you are going to need to buy some cleaning supplies. Don't worry though, its actually takes far less time to house break a dog than it did for you to be potty trained. The nice part is there are no stinky diapers to deal with here. I am going to give you what I found has been the most successful method for me and many others. You will see that the use of a crate will help you drastically with this. That is why I put crate training first. Make sure you are still keeping in mind this training is simple and very much not complicated. So here we go.

Take the dog out of the crate and straight to the door in your house. Pick one door and stick to that door. I like to hang a bell so that its low enough for the dog to hit it with a paw or their nose. When you are at the door you ring the bell. (Yes, grab the string and shake the bell) Open the door and tell the dog 'let's go potty' (or what every you want your command to be). Take the dog to the same spot in the yard every time. Give them a couple minutes to sniff and go to the bathroom. Ok, this is where it gets crazy, so hold on to something. If the dog doesn't go to the bathroom, you take them back inside. Put them back in the crate, wait 5 to 10 minutes and repeat the process. The dog doesn't get to be loose in the house until they have gone to the bathroom. When the dog poops or pees praise them and reward them. Yes, your parents made a huge deal about you going in the potty too. They probably even show pictures of you to your friends of you falling in the toilet. It's ok to be proud of your dog doing something you like. We definitely like them going to the bathroom outside.

Once the dog goes to the bathroom, go back inside. Potty time is potty time and play time is play time. Adding the bell to the routine well this will give your dog a way to connect this sound to opening the door for them to go to the bathroom. This will give your dog a way to say "hey human I got to go" without barking or scratching and jumping on your door. There is no need to try and make your dog hit the bell. The dog is watching every move you make, it will pick this up on their own. If the dog hits the bell and you take them out side and they don't use the bathroom, you take them back inside and put them in the crate. If they use the bathroom, you make a huge deal about it like you just won the lotto. Congratulations you just taught your dog to ring a bell to tell you they need to use the bath room.

Ok there you go. Stay very constant with this behavior and you will see your dog will probably be better potty trained than your kids.

Terminology

1. **Charging the Mark/Mark**. This means to mark a behavior. I use a single work. "yes". So, I say yes and give the dog a treat. So charging the mark means basically priming the pump, getting the dog to understand that that word means they are getting a reward. So, think of your mark like a picture in your dog's head. You say "YES" and pay the dog. Marking the exact behavior, the you want. Wait until the dog sits and as soon as the dog's butt touched the ground say "Yes". Once you have marked a behavior and paid the dog that behavior is over. For every mark there is a reward. The simplest way to put it 1 mark equals 1 treat. Then repeat.

2. **Luring**- This is where you are basically using the treat to guidie the dog into whatever position you want the dog to be

in. As soon as the dog is in that position, you mark and repeat. It is teasing your dog with a treat except you always give them what you are teasing them with as soon as they get to the position you want them to be in.

3. **Place-** This is exactly what it is: A place. I like to use small rugs. They are cheap and easy to move around and wash. You can use anything that is deferent than the ground around it. This gives the dog the ability to feel the place and know that they are on something. Using a place helps to build the dog's ability to target. When a dog can target and go to place. It helps the dog when you start to teach the dog to stay. You are giving the dog a place to focus to stay on. This helps the dog really understand what you want from them. You are basically telling the dog to staying right there, and the dog can now know what 'there' is, because it is an actual physical location.

4. **Sit-** I think this one is kind self-explanatory. If you lure the dogs head up with a treat the but will go down as soon as the butt touches the ground you MARK.

5. **Lay/Lie down-** I think this one is also kind self-explanatory. You can lure the dog's head up with a treat then lure the dog down to a lay position. Some dogs you will either lure down and pull slowly away making the dog crawl out, or you will slowly push the treat into them making the rock backwards. Either way that works. As soon as the dog lays completely down on the ground, you mark.

6. **Stay-** Stay means stay. In the beginning levels I never call the dog to me if I am working on stay. I want the dog to know I will come back and pay them for staying where they are. So, start with a very short distance. Even if all you do is rock back a half step, come back and "mark" and repeat. You will

eventually be able to increase the distance and time the dog will stay. You will find if you take baby steps here, the dog will learn very fast that is if they stay on this place you will come back and pay them.

7. **Here or come-** I make this into a game starting in the house or backyard. Call your dog and if they come back, they get paid. I repeat over and over again. Do not just call the dog back to you when it's time to come inside. Make this a game so the dog just knows that when it gets back to its human, they get a reward. So, call them they get to you, mark and release, and repeat.

8. **Leash Training-** While walking, say the dog' name and do a full turn. As soon as the dog gets right next to you, mark. You want to do this on the move. Having a treat ready in your hand before you get ready to turn, this will help make it easier. Repeat this over and over again. This exercise has several benefits. This will help the recall (the 'come') because the dog hears its name and will turn around. It will help with the pack structure because the dog isn't allowed to lead. The second the dog gets in front of you, change direction and put the dog behind you. Rewarding the dog when it is next to you will build the positive bubble; where the dog will want to stay because that is where the rewards are. If you have a dog that is highly stimulated, you can hold their focus by holding the just in front of the dog's nose as you walk past the distraction. As soon as you pass the distraction, mark the behavior. The key here is never stop moving. Do not try and make your dog sit when it gets excited, simply start doing turns until the dog loses interest in the stimulant and mark the dogs focus on you. You may get dizzy doing this so take it slow and keep the sessions short.

5 commands pretty simple right? I am sure you are wondering why there is no command of correction. Well there is, and corrections are absolutely part of training, just like they are part of life. I find though if you focus on your timing to reward behaviors that you want then behaviors you don't want tend to be phased out. Correction happens naturally in nature every day and are universal to anything that lives and breathes.

Men don't take offense here but women have us beat in the ability to have the perfect timing in corrections. You see women are preprogrammed to correct men and men well we are preprogramed to be corrected. Just accept the natural order and move on, you'll be happier. There are three levels of correction and they are as follows.

1. **The Look-** We all know the look. In dogs it is very easy to see, they give it to each other all the time. If one dog has a bone and the other see it. They make eye contact, give the look or stare. You can do this with your dog to correct their behavior.

2. **The Verbal-** The negative sound a lot of people use "no" . The key is it needs to be a sharp low sound that is quick and to the point. You'll see dogs growl when another dog gets too close to their food to toy.

3. **The Touch-** The touch correction is just what it is. It in no way means to hit your dog. There are several ways to apply this, some choose to use a remote collar or use pinch collars or others use choke chains. I highly suggest that if you don't have experience with a remote collar asking a profession that has real experience with introducing them and incorporating them into your training.

In this book I am not really going to focus to much on corrections. I find if you are focused on your timing of the reward then if a correction must happen you will have the timing to actually correct the exact behavior you don't want. The easiest way to apply a correction is to think of it just like the Mark but as a negative replacing the "Yes" with a "No" giving a negative mark to the behavior you don't want. So, if you told the dog to go to place and stay and the dog started to move off the place you would give the quick negative mark "no" and bring the dog back to the place and start over again. I find it helpful that if the dog breaks a behavior and you have to correct the dog immediately, show the dog exactly what you want and reward that behavior right away.

If you are going to correct a dog for a behavior, you must show them the correct behavior and reward for that behavior. Remember this a correction is just that a correction. There is no emotion in a correction. There you go, the simplest way to add corrections to you training regimen.

<u>Recall</u>

Before you dive into to your daily training logs, we need to cover recall because you aren't going to see that in your daily training goals. You are probably saying right now ok this guy is a quack who in the world doesn't put recall training in the training regimen? Well the answer to the question is: This guy.

You see the recall is built into the leash work and you will find if you do the leash work properly, saying their name and turning around it will build the muscle memory in the dog and when they hear their name, they will turn around. To take it a step further, following my belief of just living with your dog, I want to make it as easy as possible. By simply calling your dog to you and rewarding them, they will be conditioned to come to you.

The idea here is not to just call the dog to you when you want them to come inside or if they chewed on something, you need to make this fun. Call the dog to you, reward the dog and release them to go back to playing. Repeat this several times in a row in the back yard or in the house. Every single time the dog comes to you, reward the dog and release them to continue playing. This will teach your dog that coming to you is always rewarding. Coming to you is good and it doesn't mean fun is over.

You can take this out to open areas with the dog on a long leash and just walk, call the dog back to you and reward them and then keep walking. In an outdoor area, the dog may be distracted with all the smells, so you may find it use full that when you are calling the dog to come to you to start to walk backwards in the opposite directions, causing the dog to want to chase you. When the dog gets to you, reward it with praise and repeat. The dog should be on a long leash so they can't fail and run away, so be aware of how much distance you can back up from the dog. From my personal experience definitely don't do this right next to a pond with your cellphone in your pocket. If you walk backwards be aware of what's behind you.

Day 1

No Verbal Commands Yet All Behaviors Should Be Lured And Then Marked

- 10 min leash training (name, turn and Mark)

- 2 min marker training

  (name, eye contact and mark)

- 2 min marker training

  (name, eye contact and mark)

- 2 min marker training

  (name, eye contact and mark)

- 2 min marker training

  (name, eye contact and mark)

- 2 min marker training

  (name, eye contact and mark)

- 10 min leash training (Name, Turn and Mark)

Notes

<u>Day 2</u>

No Verbal Commands Yet All Behaviors Should Be Lured And Then Marked

- 10 min leash training (Name,Turn and Mark)

- 2 min marker training

  (name, eye contact and mark)

- 2 min marker training

  (name, eye contact and mark)

- 2 min marker training

  (name, eye contact and mark)

- 2 min marker training

  (name, eye contact and mark)

- 2 min marker training

  (name, eye contact and mark)

- 10 min leash training (Name, Turn and Mark)

<u>Notes</u>

Day 3

No Verbal Commands Yet All Behaviors Should Be Lured And Then Marked

- 10 min leash training (Name, Turn and Mark)

- 2 min marker training

  (name, eye contact and mark)

- 2 min marker training

  (name, eye contact and mark)

- 2 min marker training

  (name, eye contact and mark)

- 2 min marker training

  (name, eye contact and mark)

- 2 min marker training

  (name, eye contact and mark)

- 10 min leash training (Name, Turn and Mark)

Notes

Day 4

- 10 min leash training (Name Turn and Mark)

- 2 min marker training

  (name, eye contact and mark)

- 2 min marker training

  (name, eye contact and mark)

- 2 min marker training

  (name, eye contact and mark)

- 2 min marker training

  (name, eye contact and mark)

- 2 min marker training

  (name, eye contact and mark)

- 10 min leash training (Name, Turn and Mark)

Notes

<u>Day 5</u>

- 10 min leash training (Name Turn and Mark)

- 2 min marker training

  (Sit and mark)

- 2 min marker training

  (Sit and mark)

- 2 min marker training

  (Sit and mark)

- 2 min marker training

  (Lay and mark)

- 2 min marker training

  (Lay and mark)

- 10 min leash training (Name Turn and Mark)

Notes

Day 6

- 10 min leash training (Name Turn and Mark)

- 2 min marker training

  (Place, Sit and mark)

- 2 min marker training

  (Place, Sit and mark)

- 2 min marker training

  (Place, Sit and mark)

- 2 min marker training

  (Place, Lay and mark)

- 2 min marker training

  (Place, Lay and mark)

- 10 min leash training

  (Now adding stop and sit. Stop give the command sit. Mark the sit and start walking again)

<u>Notes</u>

Day 7

- 10 min leash training
  (Now adding stop and sit. Stop give the command sit. Mark the sit and start walking again)
- 2 min marker training
  (Place, Sit and mark)
- 2 min marker training
  (Place, Sit and mark)
- 2 min marker training
  (Place, Sit and mark)
- 2 min marker training
  (Place, Lay and mark)
- 2 min marker training
  (Place, Lay and mark)
- 10 min leash training (Name Turn and Mark)
  (Now adding stop and sit. Stop give the command sit. Mark the sit and start walking again)

<u>Notes</u>

Fun Challenge

Something I do with my dogs that help to build place, stay and also impulse control in the dog. Have to dog go to place while you are putting their food down. If they dog start to come off its place before your release them pick the food up before the dog get to it. Start over right away. Remember keep this very short when you start only have the dog stay for maybe a second or two then release. Build the time you have the dog stay on its place slowly. You can use "Yes" as your release here as well since you are marking the behavior and releasing them to get their food.

- **Place**

- **Stay**

- **Mark "Yes"** (this is releasing the dog from the place)

- **Eat**

If the dog breaks the stay pick the food up and start over again but shorten the length of the stay you are asking of the dog.

Adding this little drill to your meal times will help your dog learn patients and to follow your commands. There is always a reward to following your direction. If there is no reward there is no lasting behavior which will ultimately have a negative effect on your relationship.

I do this at every meal. IF you have multiple dogs, I put the food down of the oldest to youngest and release them in that order. This will help you establish the pack structure. It will also help reduce dog fights if you have young dogs eating fast them coming to try and take the other dog's food.

Day 8

- 10 min leash training
  (Now adding stop and sit. Stop give the command sit. Mark the sit and start walking again)
- 2 min marker training
  (Place, Sit and mark)
- 2 min marker training
  (Place, Sit and mark)
- 2 min marker training
  (Place, Sit and mark)
- 2 min marker training
  (Place, Lay and mark)
- 2 min marker training
  (Place, Lay and mark)
- 10 min leash training (Name Turn and Mark)
  (Start adding in the command sit then mark and start walking)

Notes

Day 9

- 10 min leash training
  (Now adding stop and sit. Stop give the command sit. Mark the sit and start walking again)
- 2 min marker training
  (Place, Sit, stay come back to dog and mark)
- 2 min marker training
  (Place, Sit, stay come back to dog and mark)
- 2 min marker training
  (Place, Sit, stay come back to dog and mark)
- 2 min marker training
  (Place, Lay, stay come back to dog and mark)
- 2 min marker training
  (Place, Lay, stay come back to dog and mark)
- 10 min leash training (Name Turn and Mark)
  (Now adding stop and sit. Stop give the command sit. Mark the sit and start walking again)

Notes

Day 10

Continue With Simple Commands

- 10 min leash training
  (Now adding stop and sit. Stop give the command sit. Mark the sit and start walking again)
- 2 min marker training
  (Place, Sit, stay come back to dog and mark)
- 2 min marker training
  (Place, Sit, stay come back to dog and mark)
- 2 min marker training
  (Place, Sit, stay come back to dog and mark)
- 2 min marker training
  (Place, Lay, stay come back to dog and mark)
- 2 min marker training
  (Place, Lay, stay come back to dog and mark)
- 10 min leash training
  (Now adding stop and sit. Stop give the command sit. Mark the sit and start walking again)

Notes

Day 11

- 10 min leash training (10 stop and "Sit" during the walk)

- 2 min marker training

  (Place, Sit, stay come back to dog and mark)

- 2 min marker training

  (Place, Sit, stay come back to dog and mark)

- 2 min marker training

  (Place, Sit, stay come back to dog and mark)

- 2 min marker training

  (Place, Lay, stay come back to dog and mark)

- 2 min marker training

  (Place, Lay, stay come back to dog and mark)

- 10 min leash training (10 Stop and "Sit" during the walk)

Notes

Day 12

Continue With Simple Commands

- 10 min leash training (10 stop and "Sit" during the walk)

- 2 min marker training

  (Place, Sit, stay come back to dog and mark)

- 2 min marker training

  (Place, Sit, stay come back to dog and mark)

- 2 min marker training

  (Place, Sit, stay come back to dog and mark)

- 2 min marker training

  (Place, Lay, stay come back to dog and mark)

- 2 min marker training

  (Place, Lay, stay come back to dog and mark)

- 10 min leash training (10 Stop and "Sit" during the walk)

<u>Notes</u>

Day 13

- 10 min leash training (10 stop and "Sit" during the walk)

- 2 min marker training

  (Place, Sit, stay come back to dog and mark)

- 2 min marker training

  (Place, Sit, stay come back to dog and mark)

- 2 min marker training

  (Place, Sit, stay come back to dog and mark)

- 2 min marker training

  (Place, Lay, stay come back to dog and mark)

- 2 min marker training

  (Place, Lay, stay come back to dog and mark)

- 10 min leash training (10 Stop and "Lay" during the walk)

Notes

Day 14

- 10 min leash training (10 stop and "Sit" during the walk)

- 2 min marker training

  (Place, Sit, stay come back to dog and mark)

- 2 min marker training

  (Place, Sit, stay come back to dog and mark)

- 2 min marker training

  (Place, Sit, stay come back to dog and mark)

- 2 min marker training

  (Place, Lay, stay come back to dog and mark)

- 2 min marker training

  (Place, Lay, stay come back to dog and mark)

- 10 min leash training (10 Stop and "Lay" during the walk)

Notes

Day 15

Now Lets Start To Kick It Up A Notch

- 10 min leash training
  (5 stops and Lays adding in the stay command walk to the end of the leash come back to the dog MARK and start walking again)
- 2 min PLACE
  (Place, Sit, stay come back to dog and mark)
- 2 min PLACE
  (Place, Sit, stay come back to dog and mark)
- 2 min PLACE
  (Place, Lay, stay come back to dog and mark)
- 2 min PLACE
  (Place, Lay, stay come back to dog and mark)
- dog and mark)
- 5 min PLACE
  (Place, Lay, stay come back to dog and mark)
- 10 min leash training
  (5 stops and Lays adding in the stay command walk to the end of the leash come back to the dog MARK and start walking again)

<u>Notes</u>

Day 16

Continue Kicking It Up A Notch

- 10 min leash training
  (5 stops and Lays adding in the stay command walk to the end
  of the leash come back to the dog MARK and start walking
  again)
- 2 min PLACE
  (Place, Sit, stay come back to dog and mark)
- 2 min PLACE
  (Place, Sit, stay come back to dog and mark)
- 2 min PLACE
  (Place, Lay, stay come back to dog and mark)
- 2 min PLACE
  (Place, Lay, stay come back to dog and mark)
  dog and mark)
- 5 min PLACE
  (Place, Lay, stay come back to dog and mark)
- 10 min leash training
  (5 stops and Lays adding in the stay command walk to the end
  of the leash come back to the dog MARK and start walking
  again)

<u>Notes</u>

Kicking the Walk Up A Notch

Now while on you are on your walks start to look for objects to have your dog get on. These are places just like using the rug in the house. As long as they are different than the ground around them. Have your dog get on them. If your dog is afraid to get on them you stand on the object. Doing this shows the dog that you are also in the game with them. You are showing them it's safe and proving to them that its ok. I never drag my dog onto anything that its afraid of.

Start with low object maybe a bench or a large rock. Point at it say "place" and lure the dog with a treat onto the place. Mark the behavior and do a couple more times and then continue on your walk. Find several challenges along your walk. This will make your time more exciting to the dog but also allow you to pretty much turn your world around you into your own personal obstacle course.

Remember to only pick sturdy objects. Always use caution if you do climb on to any object. I always say it better to be safe than sorry so if it's questionable find something else.

- Build the routine
- Place
- Stay

Go back to the dog Mark and continue on your walk and to your next challenge.

This is something I do all over town. IT will help your dog build focus on you with distractions. We cannot control the world around use. I believe we can however build strong focus and reduce the amount of stimulation it takes for our dogs to get excited. Using this simple and fun drill on your walks will help your dog build focus on you and ignore the distractions around it.

Day 17

- 10 min leash training
  (5 stops and Lays adding in the stay command walk to the end of the leash come back to the dog MARK and start walking again)
- 2 min PLACE
  (Place, Sit, stay come back to dog and mark)
- 2 min PLACE
  (Place, Sit, stay come back to dog and mark)
- 2 min PLACE
  (Place, Lay, stay come back to dog and mark)
- 2 min PLACE
  (Place, Lay, stay come back to dog and mark)
- dog and mark)
- 5 min PLACE
  (Place, Lay, stay come back to dog and mark)
- 10 min leash training
  (5 stops and Lays adding in the stay command walk to the end of the leash come back to the dog MARK and start walking again)

Notes

Day 18

Continue Kicking the Walk Up A Notch

- 10 min leash training
  (5 stops and Lays adding in the stay command walk to the end of the leash come back to the dog MARK and start walking again)
- 2 min PLACE
  (Place, Sit, stay come back to dog and mark)
- 2 min PLACE
  (Place, Sit, stay come back to dog and mark)
- 5 min PLACE
  (Place, Lay, stay come back to dog and mark)
- 5 min PLACE
  (Place, Lay, stay come back to dog and mark)
  dog and mark)
- 5 min PLACE
  (Place, Lay, stay come back to dog and mark)
- 20 min leash training
  (10 stops and Lays adding in the stay command walk to the end of the leash come back to the dog MARK and start walking again)

Notes

Day 19

Continue Kicking the Walk Up A Notch

- 10 min leash training
  (5 stops and Lays adding in the stay command walk to the end
  of the leash come back to the dog MARK and start walking
  again)
- 2 min PLACE
  (Place, Sit, stay come back to dog and mark)
- 2 min PLACE
  (Place, Sit, stay come back to dog and mark)
- 5 min PLACE
  (Place, Lay, stay come back to dog and mark)
- 5 min PLACE
  (Place, Lay, stay come back to dog and mark)
  dog and mark)
- 5 min PLACE
  (Place, Lay, stay come back to dog and mark)
- 20 min leash training
  (10 stops and Lays adding in the stay command walk to the
  end of the leash come back to the dog MARK and start
  walking again)

<u>Notes</u>

Day 20

- 20 min leash training
  (10 stops and Lays and 5 stop sits spaced out during the walk. Stand still during the behaviors for however long you want then when you are ready to start to walk again MARK and start to move again.)
- 2 min PLACE
  (Place, Sit, stay come back to dog and mark)
- 2 min PLACE
  (Place, Sit, stay come back to dog and mark)
- 5 min PLACE
  (Place, Lay, stay come back to dog and mark)
- 5 min PLACE
  (Place, Lay, stay come back to dog and mark)
  dog and mark)
- 5 min PLACE
  (Place, Lay, stay come back to dog and mark)
- 20 min leash training
  (10 stops and Lays and 5 stop sits spaced out during the walk. Stand still during the behaviors for however long you want then when you are ready to start to walk again MARK and start to move again.)

Notes

Day 21

- 20 min leash training

  (10 stops and Lays and 5 stop sits spaced out during the walk. Stand still during the behaviors for however long you want then when you are ready to start to walk again MARK and start to move again.)

- 2 min PLACE at the from door

  (Put the place with arms reach of the from door so you can pay the dog quickly. Knock on the door open close and pay the dog if it stays on the place. If the dog gets up there is no payment just repeat but be faster to close the door to catch the dog still sitting at place.

- 2 min PLACE at the from door

  (Put the place with arms reach of the from door so you can pay the dog quickly. Knock on the door open close and pay the dog if it stays on the place. If the dog gets up there is no payment just repeat but be faster to close the door to catch the dog still sitting at place.

- 5 min PLACE at the from door

  (Put the place with arms reach of the from door so you can pay the dog quickly. Knock on the door open close and pay the dog if it stays on the place. If the dog gets up there is no payment just repeat but be faster to close the door to catch the dog still sitting at place. Now start holding the door wider and wider each time. Get in the habit of saying please ignore the dog so your guest doesn't get the dog excited while it working.)

- 5 min PLACE at the from DOOR

  (Put the place with arms reach of the from door so you can pay the dog quickly. Knock on the door open close and pay the dog if it stays on the place. If the dog gets up there is no payment just repeat but be faster to close the door to catch the dog still sitting at place. Now start holding the door wider and wider each time. Get in the habit of saying please ignore the dog so your guest doesn't get the dog excited while it working.)

- 5 min PLACE

  (Put the place with arms reach of the from door so you can pay the dog quickly. Knock on the door open close and pay the dog if it stays on the place. If the dog gets up there is no payment just repeat but be faster to close the door to catch the dog still sitting at place. Now start holding the door wider and wider each time. Get in the habit of saying please ignore the dog so your guest doesn't get the dog excited while it working. Now add a person to the other side of the door. They knock you answer have the dog go to place and stay. Open the door tell the person "Come on in please ignore the dog" as they pass close the door and reward the dog. When you are practicing this if the dog gets up just close the door and repeat. The dog only gets rewarded if it completes the entire event)

- 20 min leash training

(10 stops and Lays and 5 stop sits spaced out during the walk. Stand still during the behaviors for however long you want then when you are ready to start to walk again MARK and start to move again.)

Closing Thoughts

Well now that you have completed 21 days of dog training. You may be asking yourself what now? Well the honest the truth is the only one that can answer that is you. These days and exercise can be repeated or mixed up and used at home or really anywhere you and your dog go.

My goal of this book is to ignite your desire to want more. Not just more from your dog but more from life with your dog. I have found by give even the smallest amount of success can ignite a passion that leads to so much more with your dog and life in general.

Notes

Notes

Notes

Notes

Notes

Notes

Notes

About the Author

Aaron spent 2 decades serving as a Firefighter/Medic/Police Officer. He spent the majority of this time as a Tactical Medic and an HRD K9 Handler. Through his time in public safety he found the easiest answers where usually the simplest approach.

Aaron created his training program around the bond between you and your dog. He believes that if you open communication and build the bond everything else will fall into place.

You will often hear Aaron tell people he doesn't believe he is a dog trainer anymore. He prefers more the mindset of a life coach. In today's day and age we want to label things a behavior issue when in fact it's just a dog being a dog and human interpreting the actions as a bad behavior. When you learn to communicate and read your dog what you once saw as behavior issue tends to just go away.

Made in the USA
Middletown, DE
17 July 2020